MY FIRST BOOK
GUATEMALA

ALL ABOUT GUATEMALA FOR KIDS

GLOBED
CHILDREN BOOKS

Interior and cover Design: Daniel Day
Editor: Margaret Bam

For My Sons, Daniel, David and Jude

Tikal Ruins, Guatemala

Guatemala

Guatemala is a **country**.

A country is land that is controlled by a **single government**. Countries are also called **nations, states, or nation-states**.

Countries can be **different sizes**. Some countries are big and others are small.

Panajachel, Guatemala

Where Is Guatemala?

Guatemala is located in the continent of **America**.

A continent is **a massive area of land that is separated from others by water or other natural features**.

Guatemala is situated in the **central part of America**.

Guatemala City, Guatemala

Capital

The capital of Guatemala is **Guatemala City.**

Guatemala City is situated in the southern part of the country.

Guatemala City is the largest city in Guatemala.

Great Jaguar, Tikal, Guatemala

Departments

Guatemala is divided into 22 departments

The departments of Guatemala are:

Alta Verapaz, Baja Verapaz, Chimaltenango, Chiquimula, El Progreso, Escuintla, Guatemala, Huehuetenango, Izabal, Jalapa, Jutiapa, Petén, Quetzaltenango, Quiché, Retalhuleu, Sacatepéquez, San Marcos, Santa Rosa, Sololá, Suchitepéquez, Totonicapán, and Zacapa.

Population

Guatemala has population of around **17.6 million people.**

Guatemala City is the largest and most populous city in the country, with a population of over 2.5 million people. Around 44% of the Guatemalan population lives in rural areas.

Semuc Champey, Lanquin, Guatemala

Size

Guatemala is **108,889 square kilometres** making it the 107th largest country in the world.

Guatemala is bordered by Mexico to the north and west, Belize and the Caribbean Sea to the northeast, Honduras to the east, and El Salvador to the southeast.

Languages

The official language of Guatemala is Spanish, which is spoken by the majority of the population. There are also over 20 indigenous languages spoken throughout the country, including K'iche', Kaqchikel, Q'eqchi', and Mam.

Many Guatemalans are bilingual or trilingual, speaking both Spanish and one or more indigenous languages.

Here are a few Spanish phrases

- ¿Cómo estás?- How are you?
- Mucho gusto - Nice to meet you

Santa Catalina Arch, Guatemala

Attractions

There are lots of interesting places to see in Guatemala.

Some beautiful places to visit in Guatemala are

- Tikal National Park
- Semuc Champey Natural Monument
- Santa Catalina Arch
- La Aurora Zoo
- Antigua Guatemala Central Park

History of Guatemala

Guatemala has a long and complex history that dates back thousands of years. The earliest evidence of human habitation dates back to around 12,000 BC, when hunter-gatherers first settled in the area. The Maya civilization emerged in the region around 2000 BC and flourished until the arrival of the Spanish in the 16th century.

Guatemala was colonized by the Spanish in the 16th century and after more than 300 years of Spanish rule, Guatemala gained its independence in 1821.

Guatemalan Kite Festival

Customs

Guatemala has many fascinating customs and traditions.

- Holy Week (Semana Santa) is a significant religious event in Guatemala, and the celebrations are renowned worldwide. People participate in processions, re-enacting the Passion of Christ, and making beautiful carpets made of colored sawdust, flowers, and pine needles along the procession route.
- In Guatemala, on the 1st of November every year, locals celebrate the Day of the Dead (Dia de los Muertos) by flying giant kites in cemeteries.

Music

Guatemala has a rich musical heritage that blends indigenous and Spanish influences. Some of the most popular traditional music genres in Guatemala include **marimba, son, and danzón.**

Some notable Guatemalan musicians include
- **Ricardo Arjona - One of the most successful and best-selling Latin American artists of all time**
- **Gaby Moreno - Guatemalan singer-songwriter, producer, film composer and guitarist.**
- **Hedras Ramos - Guatemalan multi-instrumentalist, specializing in guitar.**

Guatemalan Tamale

Food of Guatemala

Guatemalan cuisine is known for its fusion of Spanish, Mayan, and other indigenous cultures. Corn, beans, and chili peppers are staples in Guatemalan dishes, and they are often served with meats such as chicken, pork, or beef.

Some popular dishes in Guatemala include
- **Chiles Rellenos - Large chili peppers stuffed and then fried**
- **Tamales - Steamed corn dough stuffed with meat, vegetables, and spices**
- **Pollo en Jocón - Chicken cooked in a sauce**

Lake Peten, Guatemala

Weather

Guatemala has a **tropical climate** that is influenced by its elevation and its location near the equator.

The country experiences two seasons: a rainy season from May to October and a dry season from November to April. The rainy season brings heavy rainfall and the occasional hurricane, while the dry season is characterized by sunny days and cooler nights.

Jaguar

Animals

There are many wonderful animals in Guatemala.

Here are some animals that live in Guatemala

- Jaguar
- Margay
- Ocelot
- Cougar
- White-tailed deer
- Cedar waxwing

Monterrico Beach

Beaches

There are many beautiful beaches in Guatemala which is one of the reasons why so many people visit this beautiful country every year.

Here are some of Guatemala's beaches

- **Monterrico Beach**
- **Playa El Paredon**
- **Playa Las Lisas**
- **Champerico Beach**
- **Iztapa Beach**

Guatemala football fan

Sports

Soccer is the most popular sport in Guatemala. The sport is deeply ingrained in the culture and has a strong following among all ages.

Here are some of famous sportspeople from Guatemala

- **Érick Barrondo - Racewalking**
- **Carlos Ruiz - Football**
- **Kevin Cordón - Badminton**
- **Charles Fernandez - Athletics**

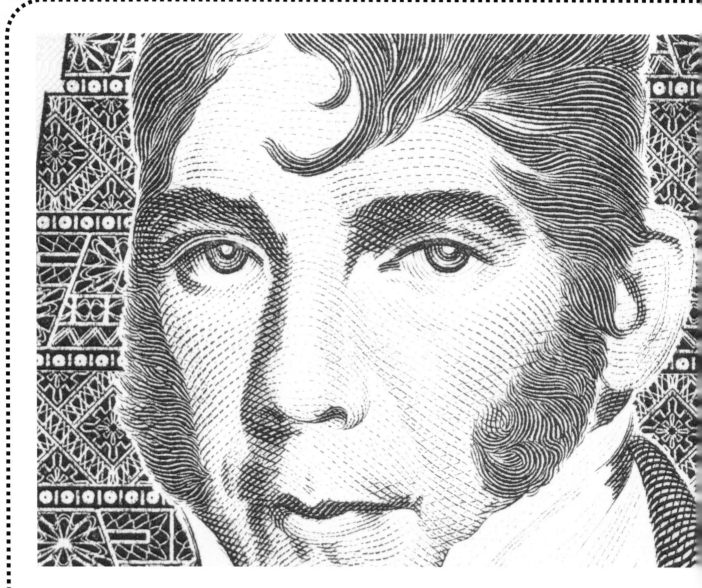

Mariano Gálvez (1794-1862)

Famous

Guatemala has been home to many notable figures in various fields.

Here are a few examples

- **José Efraín Ríos Montt - Dictator and President of Guatemala**
- **Miguel Ángel Asturias - Novelist and Journalist**
- **Oscar Isaac - Actor**
- **Mariano Gálvez - Former President of Guatemala**

Guatemalan textiles

Something Extra...

As a little something extra, we are going to share some lesser known facts about Guatemala.

- Guatemalan clothing is also significant to the country's culture. The traditional dress, or traje, is still widely worn, and each region has its unique style.
- Guatemala is home to over 30 volcanoes, three of which are still active.
- Guatemala is known for its vibrant textiles and handicrafts, which are produced by local indigenous communities.

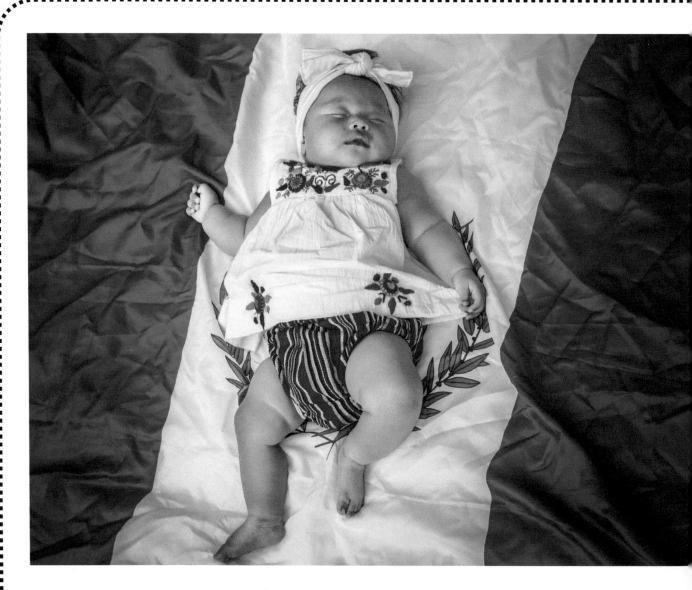

Baby on Guatemala flag

Words From the Author

We hope that you enjoyed learning about the wonderful country of Guatemala.

Guatemala is a country rich in culture and beauty, with lots of wonderful places to visit and people to meet.

We hope you continue to learn more about this wonderful nation. If you enjoyed this book, consider leaving a review!

With Love

Printed in Great Britain
by Amazon